Rain Followed Me Home

SONNETS BY
MARTIN WILLITTS JR.

GLASS LYRE PRESS

Copyright © 2023 Martin Willitts Jr.
Paperback ISBN: 978-1-941783-97-9

All rights reserved: Except for the purpose of quoting brief passages for review, no part of this book may be reproduced or transmitted in any form or by any means, electronic or mechanical, including photocopying, recording, or by any information storage and retrieval system, without permission in writing from the publisher.

Design & Layout: Steven Asmussen
Cover Art: © Physyk | Dreamstime.com
Author Photo: Linda Griggs

Glass Lyre Press, LLC
P.O. Box 2693
Glenview, IL 60025
www.GlassLyrePress.com

Rain Followed Me Home

Contents

Disquieting	1
Black and White Octaves	2
Rain	3
Always Now	4
Complaints	5
Crickets in Rain	6
Rain on a Muggy Day	7
Uncertainty	8
Listening to Rain Making Love	9
Channeling	10
Dreams are Raining	11
Why I Never Ask the Rain	12
Rain Followed Me Home	13
Water	14
Separating is Hard to Do	15
Distant Calling	16
Songbirds	17
Dusk	18
Coming in From the Rain	19
Midsummer	20
Heirloom	21
Farewell	22
Silence and Music	23
Ode to Joy (Beethoven's 5th Symphony, 4th Movement)	24
The Lessons I've Learned So Far	25
Weather Woman's Advisory	26

Discernment	27
Finding What We Have Been Waiting for All This Time	28
An Exaltation of Larks	29
Waiting for You	30
When It Rains, It Pours	31
Leaving	32
Lenticular Clouds	33
The Erie Canal	34
When Two Voices Meet	35
Medic in Rain or Shine	36
After the Funeral in the Rain	37
Tender Moments	38
Becoming Stone	39
Rain Is Spelling Words on My Window	40
Acknowledgments	41
About the Author	43

Disquieting

This present moment is — gone, gone
with sparrows into the disquieting sky — gone
white as sycamore branches before memory
releases their leaves. Gone as flattering light.
Gone as bliss and recognition of bliss. Gone,
taken away, the way rivers take silt,
depositing elsewhere. Moments are dissonant
and gorgeous, then — gone.

The pristine rains never last. It cannot rain
metaphorically everywhere with consistency.
Gravity cannot hold wind, even if wind
kisses our faces, even if it sheds sycamore leaves,
even if light folded, even if sound was shaken,
even if we clutched every moment to our chests.

Black and White Octaves

The far birds are musical notes in the sky.
I try to focus them in with a view finder.
I am trying to capture the disappearing
before they vanish. The red-orange marigold
maintains its color in black and white photographs.
Its half-tones are a part; the scattered music
becoming raindrops are another. The orange
color appears, developed even among greyscale.

A neighbor trims with a weed-whacker; grass rains.
The machine buzzes like mosquitos, at a high,
whiney-pitch, two octaves above high C.
She squares off the grass, yanks vine weed,
remakes the red-yellow snapdragons. I take photos.
Her hot-pink shorts and blue blouse emerge gray.

Rain

Listen to the rain's obsession. It's leisurely,
unstoppable remorse. Clouds squat over our house.
Rain runs back and forth like field mice.
It's monotonous.
It cancelled a parade; now, it is cartwheeling
over the fields like a girl in love with a boy
too dumb to know how lucky he can be.
Rain soaks into skin, deep-rooted bliss.

It's steady, heart-throbbing.
Even at dark noon, clouds bursts open again
and again, not offering reprieve, only revision:
rivulets of mud; sunken cars; drenched
histories; the smell of damp ewes.
A wet monarch clings to a swaying milkweed.

Always Now

Always *now* is this weather, but always going elsewhere.
Even if it does nothing, it's still something, even if it stills
like a deer staring into headlights. Always then
is the aftermath. Some might chide my noticing
the spiritual aspect. I hear their dissuading voices already.
Their words clatter-clink like hail on metal. But I listen
for the murmur of birds, the prattle of mourning doves,
the quaver of crickets, the timbering of windchimes.

I am trying to connect with the weather, to be a part
of its modulation, to understand its discord, its unrest.
Just beyond the land's edge, the straits reach out
begging hands. Distance rumbles with kettle drums.
Beyond that, we cannot see, but I know what's out there.
God is swinging in a loose hammock, quietly smiling.

Complaints

In a few minutes, unreal and raging tempestuous
roots of clouds were troubling the empty streets
with their mill of grinding winds. Great blue fingerprints
of clouds, fulfilling their promises, began
drenching rain, back and forth, having arrived this far
and having a long, long way still to go, accelerating.
This is a complaint that is answered, this complaint
without answers, this sorrow without comfort.

Accelerating life and death can happen this way:
calm to fierce, blending, impossible to discern
which is which. The seasons adapt;
however, the unanswerable problems wait
for conclusions. Maybe, the rain brings more relief;
maybe not. Those blue fingerprints smudge the sky.

Crickets in Rain

The crickets are making love. I hear their bedsprings.
Such intense, high-pitched screaming wakes the neighbors.
The high-heat excites them to extreme passion,
and when it inadvertently rains, it does not dampen
their tireless mating; they're just winding up, boisterously
proclaiming, *I'm yours, you're mine, we're forever.*
Love crosses over the fences, bounds through open windows,
stirs our hearts, and now we want to go at it,

flaming and intensely throbbing — that's the way to go —
like moths heading into a fire, burning for the lust of it.
The moonlight is cricket serenades, and we whir in response.
Love excites the weather. A rain brings cool winds,
rubbing against the window, making sounds of mating,
earth to sky, sky to stars to earth, drenching, draining.

Rain on a Muggy Day

A musky smell proceeds rain ringing on roofs.
Rain stammers over houses
with stifling humidity, sinking in our lungs.
Water evaporates as it lands.
But a robin sings its praises,
trying to tug open the curtain of clouds.
Weather sits on its haunches, nodding approvingly.
Clouds shrug their shoulders.

We need to find that quiet place
where silence enters words,
creating possibilities. We assume the worse,
but sometimes a change occurs,
and the day ecomes better than expected,
our hearts splashing excitedly in cooling rain.

Uncertainty

Think of rain. Think of it bringing a message. Think
of the rain singing, and how its melody gets closer.
Notice how the rain smiles. It is thinking.
Think of the rain as a guest. Treat it kindly.
Think of rain catching in a deer's antlers. Think of rain
being as large as forgiveness, but also less
than a gram. Think of small, wounded words.
Think how rain can start with tiny baby-steps.

A person receiving a transfusion lies near roses
someone delivered, and now the patient is too tired
to notice their bloom fading. It's a kind of courage
to watch a calendar change while minutes
become less abundant, more uncertain.
Rain concludes on the windows.

Listening to Rain Making Love

Serene clouds part, joyfully, almost holy, after rain.
When he was young, lovemaking was thunder
and lightning and torrential rain. Now that he's older,
he discovered it was better to play the softer music
on the keyboard of a lover's spine. He composes,
slower than an all-day rain, careful sonatas
enriching both of them with light brushstrokes, dabs —
how easy the melody; how actually complex.

Serene clouds part, joyfully, almost holy, after rain.
When Beethoven could not hear, he listened inside
the metronome of heart. He recalled birds, the river-
flow under ice, leaves twisting in wind before falling,
horses clopping on stone. His hands remembered lovers:
after-rain, almost holy, joyfully, parts clouds, serene.

Channeling

The heat hisses, and the lake lowers.
If rain ever comes to the rescue,
will it be too late? A few murmured sentences,
not offering relief? There's a weariness to this
silence, just a stone's throw away, a ghostly,
eerie light — hovering, a damselfly
barely making noise. Here is transmuting; but to what,
we do not know, and we do not like the unknown.

We may not know restraint. We question.
We may not appreciate it if we do not get answers.
The lake is emptying with heat, hissing.
It's light at its cruelest. It's a damselfly whisper.
It's a thread unraveling, it's the soul-light
emerging from a skull at death.

Dreams are Raining

I head towards a place
that does not exist. I take time, like rain
spattering on October leaves,
just before a settling chill.
Rain will speak to encourage a harvest, but
I never arrive. Like a cloud, I drift elsewhere.
Tell me, dreams, where are you taking me?
Tell me what I need to know.

Night after restless night, stars or leaves are
scattering. I follow the pattern, never arriving.
In my dreams, I am weather-touching everywhere.
My rain makes silence grow sadder.
It is only a little chill. It starts drizzling,
a symphony building to a volume of misery.

Why I Never Ask the Rain

You asked me why the rain visits.
No one asked before. I never asked the rain
why it established itself outside my house,
camping at my doorstep.
Maybe the rain was waiting for me
to ask what it was doing there,
silently waiting.
Maybe I should have asked. Maybe.

But maybe comes too late. Maybe comes once,
then it's over. My son will not visit me.
I cannot ask either the rain or my son
why they are gone. It's too late for that.
Ask me again about the rain. Ask about my son.
I do not expect either of them to answer...

Rain Followed Me Home

In Vietnam, it rained sidewinding.
I carried medical supplies in,
wounded men out. It rained whether
they had a missing leg, or
if the men wrote home frequently.
I swear it rained during operations.
It rained even where cranes built their nests.
It also rained if no one attacked.

I learned how to drag a wounded man
through mud into recovery. It rained
while I reached into open chest wounds.
It rained right inside more rain.
When I came home, rain followed me.
Rain kept asking for healing.

Water

A woman in Africa crosses the drought-torn desert
with a jug on her head as she searches for a hint of water.
Heat vibrates off the parched land.
Inside her head, she carries the illusion of water.
Instinct tells her water exists; all she has to do
is carry it back.
The empty jug wants the bulk of water, the texture
and splash of water's music. It knows her need.

A rich man owns so much water he wastes it,
drenches his lawn with it, spreads it over the fields,
hinting, there is more where that came from.
He drowns sorrows with it. He sprays the air recklessly.
His factory pollutes the only fresh water as he imports his.
His hands are submerged with water.

Separating is Hard to Do

We paddle out on a lake of music.
The rain is speechless,
pretending to be mute, at loss
for words, momentarily, but really
it is mostly pinpricks of rain,
easily ignored. The rain spreads thin.
The rain takes time pacing the shoreline
in contemplation.

We ease the canoe onto the creek bed.
We returned empty-handed.
Dampness soaks our bones.
We have no thought of the future,
what it might bring. Waterlogged,
we drip music, an unhurried waltz.

Distant Calling

In a remote deciduous forest, wolves sing
their moon-cycle melodies, languishing
for what they cannot have — and their restless nature
takes them between white birch, firs, and tamarack,
trying to chase moonlight, racing after it —
endless as seasons or any lost, irretrievable love.
We do not have to see the wolves to know they're there,
looing in the distance.

Their voices move, trees blocking their music,
their pitch rising and falling with the hills.
Our ears, perking, can tell which direction they're heading.
We want to follow them through the timberline,
past fire watchtowers, over loose needles and rocks,
through startled streams, mooning for love.

Songbirds

Never had so many songbirds been so silent.
Not one was spreading curving noise over the pines.
A congregation had gathered, and not one bird
erected a thin mist of music. Not one note
rustled its wings. It was eerie. Curse?
Silent worship? What caused this hush?
There were so many birds in the sky
like rainclouds, darkening, enigmatic, quiet —

a strangeness of birds, and their ambiguity
purposeful, their luxuriant colors, their frequency
of moment — why were they composed
this way? This wall of fragments and silence —
not even one wing beat? Are they insulating us?
Is there some bad news that they are encapsulating?

Dusk

Dusk bridges across the low lands as rain sweats between.
Rain walks toward us.
Sheer winds find the opening cracks of a house.
Rain slacks off a man's face.
Rain riddles the ground.
Birds chatter in this drenched sundown.
The sky's brief, green, small noises
have lightning in their veins.

Such eccentric languages! Birds frenzy and scuff,
violent translations and erasures!
Wind blows this day away into the nowhere,
disturbing horses, racing full gallop
because secrets release from the cloudbursts.
Whatever is being said is inside a cyclone.

Coming in From the Rain

Arctic terns journey thousands of miles
to their ancestral nesting areas;
why can't my son? Rain knows the imperative
to repair. I keep entering untested destinations,
but I never arrive. Rain glides in, circles;
where is my son? There are conversations
containing what no one can say to the other.
I know houses that are easier to refurbish.

We can all make something out of nothing,
until we discover what is really important.
I've held blueprints, knew what to do,
what tools I would need. But waiting for my son —
there's no instruction manual for that.
It has been raining far too long for that.

Midsummer

Not since the rain wavered over our garden
has anyone noticed the small violets
or weeded the grass between the onions
whose shoots test for rain like fingertips.
No one notices the birds blanketing the sky,
never singing. We never see the switchgrass,
although it grows in every field.
Rain arrives late; the trillium is over.

Midsummer limps along, suppressing an urge
to laugh high degrees of sweltering heat.
The hidden wants to be left alone.
The secret vocabulary of rain darkens inside
vicious clouds. The fields praise rain.
Birds distribute seeds across endless acres.

Heirloom

What appears renewed — the feverfew
close to the ground, laid out like doilies —
seems only to result in ruin: black seed casings
rubbed between my fingers crunch, fall
to spread, making white daisies
with egg-yolk centers. What appears
to be death leads toward renewal, wanting
their turn, contemplating the next chapter.

We cannot return like that. I envy the seeds.
I recycle tomato seeds of Peace Vine cherry
and baseball-sized Brandywine.
I plant inside, during winter, their starter seeds
in paper pots. Later, I rub their fuzzy stalks, smelling
tomatoes; plant; harvest; save seeds for winter.

Farewell

The rain lifts, silent as a stranger,
into the metallic-red evening sundown,
above the heat wave, tacking north
like a sailboat. The white sycamore
waves its empty fall branches: farewell.
No one should have to die at this moment.
But they do. Cancer is a bomb dropped
from miles above; something rain cannot lift.

Ducks leave the brackish river for shore
to rest on earth under the ferns.
This is not a day for someone to die,
but they do. Twilight still maintains
a certain beauty. I spent all day watching
someone dying while the rain was dying, too.

Silence and Music

Leaves shake off the last rain.
The silence afterwards sounds massive.
However, somewhere, someone tries to fill it with sounds,
shoveling small noises, with tiny, distracting impatience.
Rain had been telling a story and did not finish its ending.
It weaves and interweaves its composition
straining on its piano keys.
Our hearts want to hear it.

Our ears want to hear the rain, the thunder drumbeat,
the crack of lightning, rain clicking off leaves,
the buzzing plots of bees, tires rubbing on wet surfaces,
wipers slapping away at windshields, the unpoetic
closing umbrellas, the unraveling of people
leaving houses to welcome the sun.

Ode to Joy (Beethoven's 5th Symphony, 4th Movement)

Intended to be a philosophy of love,
this symphony become a song of intense revolution.
Its tempo is meant to jolt us out of our seat.
This is how I see you in the morning —
jubilation! But you urge me
not to talk like this — *Beethoven*
could hear you talk this way.
Your pleas fall on my deaf ears.

Invisible music catches my heart, defines it.
I do not have to hear your music moving
to know it's there. It's the coming dusk-light
or hundreds of crickets spilling out joy.
I never get enough of the singing
or the restless way we find comfort under sheets.

The Lessons I've Learned So Far

Every time I think I understand this world,
the fog empties visibility like steam from a colander.
The air rips, a chainsaw going against the grain.
Love becomes the last thing anyone can contemplate.
I could make a quilt out of this night and stars.
There goes the sun retreating into the far mountains.
Tempestuous roots of clouds trouble empty streets.
I thought the pain of experience would crush me.

Turns out, age makes the trees and me stronger.
I am more certain and assured.
Turns out, knowledge expands
like rings inside a tree. When yesterday is behind me,
somewhere the future is putting out its thumb,
hoping I'd let it hitch a ride inside me.

Weather Woman's Advisory

Today will be a humid day with high-anxiety sweltering,
a fingerprint of heat will pulse. We will move lackluster
from a door frame to a frame outside a camera.
The sunrise makes a red lipstick. The sun strains up,
and we awaken. Unwinding from our houses into heat-stink
hovering off the asphalt, we enter a sonic wave of cicadas
which jolt the rising temperature. Heat rumbles in the distance,
signaling a storm that will never arrive.

A young weatherwoman vibrantly exclaims more heat expected
in the foreseeable future. She practically bounces with pleasure,
explaining she can't wait to try out her new hot pink bikini.
Older people are advised to stay out of the killer heat,
drink plenty of fluids, stay cool, calm and collected.
Her face glows with sweat, trying not to show heat's effect.

Discernment

A thin layer of mystery covers the heart,
delicate as a spider's web, when it notices
the world has light between a leaf's veins.
What happens next will determine what follows.
Will it be a cascade of events?
Are we capable of discerning what is important
and what is not?
There are no answers to our unasked questions.

This is the way of the world —
always this endlessness, this gentleness,
even among the harshness.
We've just got to search for that calm.
We've already been told where to find it.
Maybe we can find a calm place after all.

Finding What We Have Been Waiting for All This Time

The troubling weather arrived and stayed and stayed
and stayed until it fizzled-out rain and snow.
The clouds emptied their sheet music to begin again.
A few clouds moved like a funeral procession.
Light cracked under the doorway of morning.
The blue, miniature speedwells could be buttons
for a woman's dress. Laughter inches forward,
as aimless as ocean waves.

The bunchberry is consoled. Chairs wait
for someone to discuss peace. Love arrives,
mist-spray reaching landfall.
People stop whatever they are doing,
drop their silences like baggage, recall
the world was this happy once before.

An Exaltation of Larks

(term for a gathering of larks, also their collective sounds)

The ground ripples with lark in field-stubble,
matching the bare earth, stirring the world
through high, tinkling music. More aggregations
numbering in the hundreds swirl in winter skies.
They praise the air, the land, even
the dry, dead grass nesting between snow melt.
They exalt intensely. They are jazz notes from Miles Davis
punctuating what is felt, birthing the cool, the extravagant.

We should be so draped in joy, with such be-bop happiness.
Larks understand it is better to congregate to celebrate,
to let loose blasts of flare and tribute — all collaboration,
raw interpretation, innovation — snowflakes of music notes;
acclaiming and proclaiming without restraint;
fierce jubilation in the harshest, coldest times.

Waiting for You

Just like a good steady rain,
handwritten by the blue jay's flight,
the edges of the world need you.
I am aware of the heartbreak
behind the rain's curtain.
The river banks swell, the ground
saturates, run-offs follow
a downward slope as arpeggios.

The clouds squeeze tight.
Rain crunches on roofs, abundantly,
but, like love or pain, cannot last forever.
There is no sound inside the rain
that is not you. A heart may be breakable,
but the door is unlatched, waiting for you.

When It Rains, It Pours

A broom whispers a shadow away.
A red shirt hangs on a wash line with an apology.
When I open a letter, wind comes out,
skirts across the polished floor.
Two pink, lacy, hollyhock flowers wake up.
A dog opens one eye when a fox sneaks a mile away.
A bird's piccolo twitters happiness with steamy intent,
flittering in swatches of light.

A bumblebee drifts nonchalantly over a pink tulip, in
and out daffodils, past purple violets, trying to decide.
It wobbles slightly off-course, taking a little from each,
hunger-driven in love.
Bumblebees know about reciprocal-sharing.
We are in our lover's arms, drenched in this music.

Leaving

Rain hums in a reddish-orange chrysanthemum,
singing about tomorrow, recovering stars,
the meticulous sunrises, the boat of love arriving,
silence taken by geese, lyrics of rivers,
the ecstatic cursive written by looping swifts
while their wings sound like applause.
Today rises from immersion,
a developed photographs from emulsion.

The rain says goodbye, a vapor trail of regret,
drifting beyond the hillock, into a vanishing trick.
Feverfew dollies of egg-yolk, yellow centers —
have a cure for whatever ails us. Light rings its doorbell.
There are offerings of a second chance.
Our hands are birds discovering flight.

Lenticular Clouds

Lenticular clouds form over cone-shaped hilltops.
When air scales those heights, not musically,
but hand-over-hand, rising and descending
in atmospheric waves, frequency pitches.
After the temperature reaches the right conditions
of lowering to dewpoint, in octaves,
an undeniable music, these clouds appear as flying saucers,
people frantically calling to report an invasion.

The alien sun sets, rippling burgundy solos,
a steep wave-length, purging-longing.
We are saturated. My breath straggles up the stairs,
to find tenderness, a mist revealing my wife.
I enter into her arms at sundown, a room
full of remembrance, a story of impulsive storms.

The Erie Canal

In wine-dark purpling at dusk, quiet
settles among taut trees. Green algae cling
to stillness. Cottonwoods reflect upon
water, not in a hurry to rush. Traveling geese
float, wearing their nighttime black masks,
sleeping in ambient light. Canal water
ripples like a dog chasing a cat
in dreams. Its brackish water is in stasis.

Overgrown by weeds, rounded up by cattails,
the canal yawns. Peepers splash serenades,
easing my solitary boat. An applause of fireflies
flickers after softening edges of rain pass.
Birds, frogs, crickets — all succumb to rest.
My boat rocks its own cradle in a tender rain.

When Two Voices Meet

We could say the clouds unraveled
to see clear across county lines. We could say
the door of the heart always opens
to urgent messages. This strange feeling
taps on our shoulders.
When two voices travel distances
trying to bridge a gap,
it is all in the timing.

It's all about reaching out before it is too late.
It's all about reassuring someone else
we are listening. It's about raining love.
Sometimes the heart feels a hard weight,
and it needs to release guilt before dying.
Even an extended music chord knows an end.

Medic in Rain or Shine

And when the winds come from the hills,
I do not mind if they bring the rains
along for the ride. The sky is reflective-
black as the Vietnam Memorial Wall
where my face, mirrored, has names written on it.
My name, thankfully, is not on the wall.
It could have been engraved. I was that close.
I checked-twice. War and bullets were inches apart.

People were rubbing names on the wall.
Someone asked if I knew anyone there,
pointing to the massive list. I pulled out many
of those names, feeling failure, seeing them die.
I heard bullets and rain, almost the same,
with red skies exploding.

After the Funeral in the Rain

We forget our promises never to forget.
Months after a car caravan followed the black hearse
and we walked in silence under opened umbrellas
carrying single, long-stem roses, life went on anyway.
We forgot, eventually, the way gravel and grass felt.
Our world collapsed like the rain, briefly, and still
the forget-me-nots arrive every spring.
We forgot to remember, because birds sing sweetly daily.

There are days when memory lessens. We hold on
the stillness. We mumble a prayer and forget.
We lose that last touch we promised to cherish.
All we have now is guilt after memory lapses
and interruptions elbow in. Like geese, memory flies.
We change bedsheets, fix dinner, admire another sundown.

Tender Moments

There is much to love in this world,
and much we never saw but can guess
easily has to be spectacular
in a quieting rain on the violets.
A robin touches down, hops across the wet grass,
searching for grubs or worms rising to the surface.
These soft moments urge us
to nap in the Brahm's lullaby rain.

If we care to look at these moments,
we sense a blush of sun behind the cloud's curtains,
rain falling just enough, not more,
not less; a crow cocking its blue-black head
suspicious of the silence; or
violets returning every year.

Becoming Stone

The rain clacks on stones, chanting
as carefully as snowmelt. Perhaps, it rains
from the Pleiades: seven doves or sisters fleeing.
A heron stands near water's edge on the largest rock,
while rain deepens the experience of meditation.
The heron listens to the messages, the sacred
chants telling the heron when the world ends.
The rain takes its time telling this news.

The heron cocks its head towards words.
I need to learn the pace of stones,
before I'd understand the slowed-down
words of rocks from the Creation of stars:
Time is less than one rain drop; what are you doing,
when you could be merging with life?

Rain Is Spelling Words on My Window

Entire galaxies might not have rain.
On parts of earth, rain falls parched before it lands.
Images of rain fall desperately
on the endless geometry of places that it never touches.
When rain never reaches, it has no mystical power.
Rain hesitates trying to avoid whatever it is about to say,
can't name the places it wants to go.
We want to know what the rainstorm is trying to tell us.

Of all the musical notes spilling out of the clouds,
not one has a chord striking a melody in our hearts.
Rain rushes silence into our waiting arms.
It rains, but the sun is out.
The bobwhite asked for and received both,
glorifying both, even the timeless pauses between.

Acknowledgments

My sincere thanks to the editors of the following publications in which these poems, some in earlier versions, first appeared:

Alexandria Quarterly: "Heirloom"

Autumn Sky Poetry Daily: "Disquieting," "Songbirds," "Uncertainty," "Waiting for You"

Black Poppy Review: "Separating is Hard to Do"

Blue Nib: "Discernment"

Broadkill River Review: "Coming in from the Rain"

Califragile: "Channeling"

Cloudburst Council Anthology: "Tender Moments"

Comstock Review: "Crickets in Rain," "Distant Calling"

Good Works Review: "Medic in Rain or Shine"

Night Garden Journal: "Farewell"

Pirene's Fountain: "Black and White Octaves"

Poetry Matters Project (Contest Finalist): "An Exaltation of Larks"

Poppy Road Review: "Becoming Stone," "Midsummer"

Red Earth Review: "Listening to Rain Making Love"

Shelia-Na-Gig: "Always Now"

Silver of Stone: "Ode to Joy"

Stone Canoe: "The Erie Canal"

Survival Anthology: "The Lessons I've Learned So Far," "Rain Followed Me Home"

Trajectory: "Complaints," "Why I Never Ask the Rain"

About the Author

Martin Willitts Jr is a retired Librarian living in Syracuse, New York. He was nominated for 15 Pushcart and 13 Best of the Net awards. Winner of the 2012 *Big River Poetry Review's* William K. Hathaway Award; 2013 Bill Holm Witness Poetry Contest; 2014 Broadsided award; 2014 Dylan Thomas International Poetry Contest; Rattle Ekphrastic Challenge, June 2015, Editor's Choice; *Rattle* Ekphrastic Challenge, Artist's Choice, November 2016, Stephen A. DiBiase Poetry Prize, 2018; Editor's Choice, *Rattle Ekphrastic Challenge*, December, 2020. He won a Central New York Individual Artist Award and provided "Poetry on The Bus" which had 48 poems in local buses including 20 bi-lingual poems from 7 different languages.

Martin Willitts Jr has 25 chapbooks including the *Turtle Island Quarterly* Editor's Choice Award, "The Wire Fence Holding Back the World" (Flowstone Press, 2017), plus 21 full-length collections including the Blue Light Award 2019, "The Temporary World." His new full-length is *Harvest Time* (Deerbrook Press, 2021). Forthcoming books include *Not Only the Extraordinary are Exiting the Dream World* (Flowstone Press, 2021), and *All Wars Are the Same War* (FutureCycle Press, 2022). He is an editor for the Comstock Review and Judge for the New York State Fair Poetry Contest.

Glass Lyre Press

exceptional works to replenish the spirit

Glass Lyre Press is an independent literary publisher interested in technically accomplished, stylistically distinct, and original work. Glass Lyre seeks diverse writers that possess a dynamic aesthetic and an ability to emotionally and intellectually engage a wide audience of readers.

Glass Lyre's vision is to connect the world through language and art. We hope to expand the scope of poetry and short fiction for the general reader through exceptionally well-written books, which evoke emotion, provide insight, and resonate with the human spirit.

Poetry Collections
Poetry Chapbooks
Select Short & Flash Fiction
Anthologies

www.GlassLyrePress.com

www.ingramcontent.com/pod-product-compliance
Lightning Source LLC
Chambersburg PA
CBHW030201100526
44592CB00009B/397